365
Prayer Points
to Claim a
Wonderful Year

Gbenga Showunmi

365 Prayer Points to Claim a Wonderful Year

Copyright © 2022 by **Gbenga Showunmi**

ISBN: 978-1-957809-39-7

Printed in the United States of America. All rights reserved solely by the author. This book or parts thereof may not be reproduced in any form, stored in a retrieval system, or transmitted in any form by any means - electronic, mechanical, photocopy. Unless otherwise noted, Bible quotations are taken from the Holy Bible, New King James Version. Copyright 1982 by Thomas Nelson, Inc., publishers. Used by permission.

Cornerstone Publishing
A Division of Cornerstone Creativity Group LLC
Phone: +1(516) 547-4999
info@thecornerstonepublishers.com
www.thecornerstonepublishers.com

To order bulk of this book or to contact the author please email:
info@thecornerstonepublishers.com

How to Use this Book

There is flexibility in using this prayer manual. Unlike the *100 Prayer Points to Claiming a Wonderful Year*, this manual is divided into 52 prayer topics, with an average of seven prayer points per topic. This means that you have the choice of using it as:

- a daily or weekly prayer all through the year or

- you may decide to pray all at once, until you exhaust the prayer points.

Contents

How to Use this Book..3

Exerpt from *100 Prayer Point for Claiming a Wonderful Year*!..7

1. Thanksgiving..11
2. Consecration...13
3. New Things...15
4. Divine Guidance and Leading.................................17
5. Abundant Grace..19
6. Help from Above...21
7. Anointed to Succeed..23
8. Fruitfulness..25
9. Wealth Transfer..27
10. Courage..29
11. Divine Wisdom..31
12. Grace..33
13. Victory over Enemies...35
14. Victory over Failure..37
15. Supernatural Favor...39
16. Victory Over the Forces of Resistance and Opposition..41

17. Innovative and Winning Idea......................43
18. Open Doors of Opportunities.....................45
19. It's My Season of Elevation and Promotion.........47
20. Enlarge My Coast................................49
21. Victory over Spirit of Error....................51
22. Divine Guidance.................................53
23. Divine Connections..............................55
24. No More Profitless Labor........................57
25. Give Me the Nations.............................59
26. Financial Breakthrough..........................61
27. The Spirit of Excellence........................63
28. Spiritual Discernment 65
29. Harvest...67
30. Divine Speed and Acceleration...................69
31. My Star Must Shine..............................71
32. Showers of Blessings............................73
33. Crushing Barriers and Strongholds...............75
34. Deliverance from Fear...........................77
35. Evil Attacks 79
36. Healing in my Body..............................81
37. Intimacy with God 83
38. Victory for my Head 85
39. Prayer for My Children..........................87
40. Family Issues...................................89
41. Marital Issues for Singles......................91

42. Breaking Curses and Spells..93
43. Dominion Over Circumstances......................95
44. Divine Protection...97
45. Restorations..99
46. Overflow of Provision...101
47. Supernatural Manifestations and Results.............103
48. Revival..105
49. Commanding Greatness.................................107
50. Anointing of the Holy Spirit........................109
51. No More Shame..111
52. A New Song..113

Exerpt from

100 Prayer Point for Claiming a Wonderful Year!

1. Thank You, Lord, for Your love, kindness and faithfulness toward my loved ones and I.

2. Thank You for giving my loved ones and I another year of power, grace and fulfillment.

3. Thank You, Lord Jesus, for the opportunity to live to see another great year full of hope.

4. This year, Lord, I rededicate my life to You; wash me, Lord, with Your precious blood, and forgive all my sins, disobedience and rebellions.

5. Father, grant me grace to live a life pleasing and glorifying You this year and for the rest of my life. In Jesus' Name, Amen.

6. Father, I pray for the salvation, deliverance and freedom of all my family members from sin and darkness. In Jesus' Name, Amen.

7. Almighty God, renew my strength like the eagle to accomplish all Your plans and purposes for my life this year. In Jesus' Name, Amen.

8. Father, show me Your ways and direct all my paths as I seek Your face for great experiences this year. In Jesus' Name, Amen.

9. Father, I declare that this year shall be better, brighter and bigger for my loved ones and I. In Jesus' Name, Amen.

10. Father, I reject all negativities from last year; they shall not define me this year and beyond. In Jesus' Name, Amen.

11. Father, I demand restoration of whatever the devil has stolen from me last year. I demand the restoration of my peace, joy, prosperity and health, in Jesus' Name!

12. Father, all good things You have started in my life last year shall make progress and be perfected this year, in Jesus' Name. Amen.

13. Father, I receive supernatural faith to do greater works and accomplish great feats this year, in Jesus' Name. Amen.

14. Father, let there be outpouring of Your Holy Spirit in my life; anoint me specially this year to advance Your kingdom. In Jesus' Name, Amen.

15. Holy Spirit, the Spirit of wisdom and knowledge, guide me into greatness, victory and breakthrough this year, in Jesus' Name. Amen.

16. Spirit of the living God, make all things new and give me freshness of life, in Jesus' Name. Amen.

17. Father, this year, I receive spiritual revival, growth, and faithfulness in my relationship with You, in Jesus' Name. Amen.

18. Father, I declare that I shall not have any regrets whatsoever this year. All things will work together for my good, progress and prosperity. In Jesus' Name, Amen.

19. Lord, this year, I declare that instead of shame, I shall have double honor; instead of

disappointment, I shall have new glorious appointment, in Jesus' Name. Amen.

20. Father, this year, I shall be elevated, promoted, and celebrated, in Jesus' Name. Amen.

21. Father, this year, I receive power and anointing to break through limitations, barriers and barricades in Jesus' Name. Amen.

22. Father, this year I receive the Excellent Spirit to excel and succeed in all my endeavors, in Jesus' Name. Amen.

23. Father, I receive grace this year to make up with great speed all my wasted years, and to accomplish more than I have ever imagined. In Jesus' Name, Amen.

24. Father Lord, this year, direct me to those who really matter to my greatness in life. In Jesus' Name, Amen.

25. Father, this year, send help to me. Let me never be stranded, frustrated and helpless. In Jesus' Name, Amen.

Note: You can get this powerful, and complete version of *100 Prayer Points for Claiming a Wonderful* on Amazon.com.

1

Thanksgiving

Psalms 100:4-5

Enter his gates with thanksgiving
and his courts with praise;
give thanks to him and praise his name.
For the Lord is good and his love endures forever;
his faithfulness continues through all generations

1. Thank You, Lord, for all your mighty works in my life.

2. Thank You for keeping, protecting, and preserving me.

3. Thank You, Lord, for Your guidance and instruction in the right direction.

4. Lord, I thank You for my family and loved ones all through the years.

5. Father, I thank You for blessing my job, career and ministry.

6. Thank you, Lord, for all the people in my life whom You have positioned to help me.

7. Thank You, Jesus, for fighting all my battles - visible and invisible.

8. Father, thank You for giving me another year, another opportunity.

9. Thank You, Lord, for good health, strength and grace.

10. Blessed be Your name, forever.

2

Consecration

Isaiah 59:1-3

Behold, the Lord's hand is not shortened,
That it cannot save;
Nor His ear heavy,
That it cannot hear.
But your iniquities have separated you from your God;
And your sins have hidden His face from you,
So that He will not hear.
3 For your hands are defiled with blood,
And your fingers with iniquity;
Your lips have spoken lies,
Your tongue has muttered perversity.

1. Lord, this year, I present myself to You as Your son/daughter. Please have mercy on me.

2. This year, Lord, I rededicate my life to You; wash me, Lord, with Your precious blood, and forgive all my sins, disobedience and rebellions.

3. Father, grant me grace to live a life pleasing and glorifying You, this year and for the rest of my life. In Jesus' Name, Amen.

4. Father, I pray for the salvation, deliverance and freedom of all my family members from sin and darkness. In Jesus' Name, Amen.

5. Lord, give me a clean heart and clean hands to love You and to serve You more.

6. Father, let the power of sin be completely shattered in my life, in Jesus' Name.

7. Lord, this year, I receive the garment of holiness and righteous in Jesus.

3

New Things

Isaiah 43:18-19

"Forget the former things;
do not dwell on the past.
See, I am doing a new thing!
Now it springs up; do you not perceive it?
I am making a way in the wilderness
and streams in the wasteland.

1. Father, I declare a new beginning in the right direction this year for my family and me. In Jesus' Name, Amen.

2. Spirit of the living God, make all things new and give me freshness of life. In Jesus' Name, Amen.

3. Father, I declare that this year shall be better, brighter and bigger for my loved ones and I. In Jesus' Name, Amen.

4. Father, I reject all negativities from last year; they shall not define me this year and beyond. In Jesus' Name, Amen.

5. Father, I demand restoration of whatever the devil has stolen from me last year. I demand restoration of my peace, joy, prosperity and health in Jesus' Name. Amen!

6. Father, all the good things You started in my life last year shall make progress and be perfected this year. In Jesus' Name, Amen.

7. Father, I receive supernatural faith to do greater works and accomplish great feats this year. In Jesus' Name, Amen.

8. Father, all Your promises for my life this year shall be fulfilled in grand style. In Jesus' Name, Amen.

4

Divine Guidance and Leading

Proverbs 3:5-6

Trust in the Lord with all your heart
and lean not on your own understanding;
in all your ways submit to him,
and he will make your paths straight.

1. Father, show me Your ways and direct all my paths as I seek Your face for great experiences this year. In Jesus' Name, Amen.

2. Father, guide me to the right place at the right time. In Jesus' Name, Amen.

3. Holy spirit, let me walk in discernment this year like never before. In Jesus' Name, Amen.

4. Lord, I reject all evil, demonic and negative influences over my decisions this year in Jesus' Name.

5. Father, hold my right hand this year and lead me to my wealthy place. In Jesus' Name, Amen.

6. Father, let Your light shine on my path this year; let me not walk in the dark. In Jesus' Name, Amen.

7. Lord, I block all distractions and the spirit of inconsistency in my life this year in Jesus' Name.

5

Abundant Grace

2 Corinthians 9:8

And God is able to make all grace abound toward you, that you, always having all sufficiency in all things, may have an abundance for every good work.

1. Thank You, Lord, for answering prayers.
2. Lord, give me grace that matches all Your promises for my life this year. In Jesus' Name, Amen.
3. Father, by Your grace, I shall overcome all challenges and circumstances this year. In Jesus' Name, Amen.
4. Lord, endow me with grace to do the impossible, and to carry out Your purpose in Jesus' Name.

5. Father, let all mountainous problems before me be scattered and shattered. In Jesus' Name, Amen.

6. Father, this year, I receive abundant grace in all areas of my life to disgrace all situations that attempt to disgrace me. In Jesus' Name, Amen.

7. Father, let Your grace speak for me in great places, and grant me access to greatness. In Jesus' Name, Amen.

6

Help from Above

Psalm 121:1-2

I will lift up my eyes to the hills—
From whence comes my help?
My help comes from the Lord,
Who made heaven and earth.

Hebrews 13:5-6

Let your conduct be without covetousness; be content with such things as you have. For He Himself has said, "I will never leave you nor forsake you." So we may boldly say:
"The LORD is my helper;
I will not fear.
What can man do to me?"

1. Father, thank You for always defending, supporting and helping me in everything I do.

2. Lord, I look up to You; let me not be helpless and hopeless this year. In Jesus' Name, Amen.

3. Father, send help to me in every direction I turn this year. In Jesus' Name, Amen.

4. Father, this year, I shall not be stranded, frustrated or helpless. In Jesus' Name, Amen.

5. Lord, hold me with Your mighty hand all through this year; let me not fall; let me not fail. In Jesus' Name, Amen.

6. Father, let those who strive to thwart me this year perish and be as nothing. In Jesus' Name, Amen.

7. Lord, use the influence of others to lead me to greatness and prosperity. In Jesus' Name, Amen.

7

Anointed to Succeed

Psalm 1:3 (NCV)

They are strong, like a tree planted by a river.
The tree produces fruit in season,
and its leaves don't die.
Everything they do will succeed.

1. Thank You, Lord, for always hearing my prayers.

2. Today, I stand in the authority of the word of God and declare that I will succeed, I will prosper, and I will be great this year, together with my loved ones. In Jesus' Name, Amen.

3. Lord, I receive all grace and abilities to succeed

in all my projects and endeavors this year. In Jesus' Name, Amen.

4. All powers of failure in my life and family, be destroyed now. In Jesus' Name, Amen.

5. I and my loved ones are anointed to succeed by the Holy Spirit. In Jesus' Name, Amen.

6. I decree and declare that every effort of the enemy to limit my success this year will be frustrated and annulled. In Jesus' Name, Amen.

7. I declare that nothing shall fail in my hands this year. Whatever my hand touches shall succeed. In Jesus' Name, Amen.

8. The work of my hand is blessed.

8

Fruitfulness

Genesis 1:28

Then God blessed them, and God said to them, "Be fruitful and multiply; fill the earth and subdue it; have dominion over the fish of the sea, over the birds of the air, and over every living thing that moves on the earth."

1. Lord, thank You for answering all my prayers.

2. I take authority in the name of Jesus against the demons, principalities, and powers of darkness ruling in the realm of unfruitfulness in my life; I command them to be removed now. In Jesus' Name, Amen.

3. My father and my Lord, You created me and commanded me to be fruitful; therefore, I reject any kinds of unfruitfulness in my life this year. In Jesus' Name, Amen.

4. Father Lord, I receive by fire the grace to be productive in my marital life, spiritual life, financial life, and intellectual life this year. In Jesus' mighty Name, Amen.

5. Father, let any area of my life experiencing emptiness be full, In Jesus' Name, Amen. I decree that the siege of barrenness and emptiness is completely over in my life. In Jesus' Name, Amen.

6. Father, lay Your powerful hand upon my spouse and me; let Your power of productivity manifest through us. In Jesus' Name, Amen.

7. The God that remembered Hannah, Abraham and Sarah, remember me and change my story to glory; change my barrenness to fruitfulness in the name of Jesus.

9

Wealth Transfer

Isaiah 60:5

Then you shall see and become radiant, And your heart shall swell with joy; Because the abundance of the sea shall be turned to you, The wealth of the Gentiles shall come to you.

1. Thank You, Lord, for answering my prayers.
2. Thank You, Lord, for giving me the power to attain wealth.
3. Father, I receive the ability and grace to prosper this year. In Jesus' Name, Amen.
4. Lord, wealth and riches shall be in my house this year. In Jesus' Name, Amen.

5. Lord, command the transfer of wealth of the gentiles to me by favor. In Jesus' Name, Amen.

6. Father, the earth is the Lord's and its fullness; let heaven open and release blessings upon me this year so unlimited that I will not have enough room to contain them. In Jesus' Name.

7. O God, this year, I step into my wealthy place this year; I shall not be poor again in my life. In Jesus' Name, Amen.

10

Courage

Joshua 1:5-9

No man shall be able to stand before you all the days of your life; as I was with Moses, so I will be with you. I will not leave you nor forsake you. Be strong and of good courage, for to this people you shall divide as an inheritance the land which I swore to their fathers to give them. Only be strong and very courageous, that you may observe to do according to all the law which Moses My servant commanded you; do not turn from it to the right hand or to the left, that you may prosper wherever you go. This Book of the Law shall not depart from your mouth, but you shall meditate in it day and night, that you may observe to do according to all that is written in it. For then you will make your way prosperous, and then you will have good success. Have I not commanded you? Be strong and of good courage; do not be afraid, nor be dismayed, for the Lord your God is with you wherever you go."

1. Lord, I thank You for all the blessings and favor in my life.

2. Father, let my life demonstrate Your power and glory this year. In Jesus' Name, Amen.

3. By the power of the Holy Spirit, I receive boldness and courage to possess my possessions this year. In Jesus' Name, Amen.

4. I refuse to be afraid; I face my destiny and greatness this year with courage. In Jesus' Name, Amen.

5. Father, every force that wants to paralyze my courage must be removed and disgraced. In Jesus' Name, Amen.

6. Lord, strengthen my faith to trust You more than ever before. In Jesus' Name, Amen.

7. Father, grant me giant faith to take up giant goals this year. In Jesus' Name, Amen.

11

Divine Wisdom

James 1:5

If any of you lacks wisdom, let him ask of God, who gives to all liberally and without reproach, and it will be given to him.

1. Lord, thank You for all answers to my prayers. In Jesus' Name, Amen.

2. Father, I thank You; You are the pure wisdom from above. Thank You for guiding my life so far.

3. Father, I thank You for Your Holy Spirit; the Spirit of wisdom, knowledge and understanding.

4. Father, baptize me with the Spirit of wisdom.

5. Father, kill the manifestation of foolishness and ignorance in my life. In Jesus' Name, Amen.

6. Father, You use the foolish things of this world to confound the wise. Father, turn every plot of the enemies against my life to foolishness. In Jesus' Name, Amen.

7. Father, I reject every worldly counsel arranged from the pit of hell against me, and it will be destroyed. In Jesus' Name, Amen.

8. Oh Lord, give me creative wisdom above my competitors. In Jesus' Name, Amen.

9. Father, release into my life extraordinary wisdom that will show and bring forth Your glory in my life.

12

Grace

2 Corinthians 9:8

And God is able to make all grace abound toward you, that you, always having all sufficiency in all things, may have an abundance for every good work.

1. Father, I thank You for grace at work already in my life.

2. Father, let Your grace be multiplied upon my life and grant me speed this year. In Jesus' Name, Amen.

3. Lord, by Your grace, I will be very accomplished and fulfilled in everything I do this year. In Jesus' Name, Amen.

4. Jesus, I receive Your grace to overcome my challenges this year.

5. Father, let Your glory fall on me; let all those who seek to mock me be ashamed. In Jesus' Name, Amen.

6. Lord, release upon me grace that makes me great. In Jesus' Name, Amen.

7. Father, let me soar like the eagles on Your wings of grace this year. In Jesus' Name, Amen.

13

Victory over Enemies

Psalm 25:2

To You, O Lord, I lift up my soul.
O my God, I trust in You;
Let me not be ashamed;
Let not my enemies triumph over me.

1. Lord, I thank You for answering my prayers. In Jesus' Name, Amen.

2. Father, I decree and declare victory over all enemies of progress, in Jesus' Name.

3. O God, all evil gatherings against life and my destiny shall scatter. In Jesus' Name, Amen.

4. I am born of God; I will be victorious over my enemies in Jesus' Name.

5. Father, break down all networks conspirings against my me and loved ones. In Jesus' Name, Amen.

6. This year, all those who seek my downfall shall be ashamed. In Jesus' Name, Amen.

7. This year, I will shout a shout of victory and triumph over the mockers of my life. In Jesus' Name, Amen.

14

Victory over Failure

1 John 5:4

For whatever is born of God overcomes the world. And this is the victory that has overcome the world—our faith.

1. Thank You, Lord, for putting me on the path of success.

2. Father, today, I arrest every spirit of failure in my life, career and ministry in Jesus' Name.

3. O God, this year, I declare victory over all the forces that held me down from succeeding. In Jesus' Name, Amen.

4. Lord, this year, I destroy every demonic operation attempting to degrade my value and effectiveness. In Jesus' Name, Amen.

5. Father, this year, I pull down strongholds of bad luck, disappointment and failure in my life in Jesus' Name.

6. I declare that I refuse to be a failure in my life. This is my year to succeed in grand style. In Jesus' Name, Amen.

7. Father, all my decisions and actions shall not lead to failure. In Jesus' Name, Amen.

15

Supernatural Favor

Psalms 5:12

For You, O Lord, will bless the righteous;

With favor You will surround him as with a shield.

1. Lord of mercy, let Favor single me out for the miraculous this year in Jesus' Name.
2. Father, perfume my life and my loved ones with the aroma of favor. Let my life attract goodwill. In Jesus' Name, Amen.
3. By favor, let those who have rejected me promote and celebrate me. In Jesus' Name, Amen.

4. Father, this is my year of favor, let it last forever. In Jesus' Name, Amen.

5. Lord, this year, let me be preferred above my competitors. In Jesus' Name, Amen.

6. I declare that the favor of God will locate me everywhere I go. In Jesus' Name, Amen.

7. Through high favor, Mary gave birth to the king of glory; Lord, baptize me with high favor, and let me leave a mark for my generation.

16

Victory Over the Forces of Resistance and Opposition

Genesis 26:22

22 And he moved from there and dug another well, and they did not quarrel over it. So he called its name [a] Rehoboth, because he said, "For now the Lord has made room for us, and we shall be fruitful in the land."

1. Father, thank You for Your strength and Your might that carries me always.

2. God Almighty, let all powers resisting my rising crumble now in Jesus' Name.

3. Lord of hosts, every strong man that will not let me move forward this year will fall. In Jesus' Name, Amen.

4. Father, deliver me from stronger people; paralyze their plans and efforts over my life. In Jesus' Name, Amen.

5. Today, I break and destroy all barriers and barricades erected against my life and greatness. In Jesus' Name, Amen.

6. All opposition, like Goliath and the walls of Jericho, will fall and be scattered in Jesus' Name. Amen.

17

Innovative and Winning Idea

Job 32:8

*But there is a spirit in man,
And the breath of the Almighty gives him understanding.*

Proverbs 8:12 (KJV)

I wisdom dwell with prudence, and find out knowledge of witty inventions.

1. Father, inspire me with great ideas (that will take me from where I am to where I ought to be in my ministry and career) and strategies to execute them in Jesus' Name.

2. Father, let my heavens be opened perpetually. This year, I shall not lack flow in inspiration and ideas. In Jesus' Name, Amen.

3. This year, release upon me by the Holy Spirit an innovative and winning idea. Let everything that represents me stand out this year. In Jesus' mighty Name, Amen.

4. Lord, I receive the grace this year to make a lasting impact in my chosen career, business and ministry. In Jesus' Name, Amen.

5. Father, You are the creator of the earth; give me creative ideas that would advance and bring me to prominence this year. In Jesus' Name, Amen.

6. Father, renew my mind for new things in Jesus' Name.

7. This year, I declare that I am leading in my sphere of influence. In Jesus' Name, Amen.

18

Open Doors of Opportunities

Revelation 3:8

"I know your works. See, I have set before you an open door, and no one can shut it; for you have a little strength, have kept My word, and have not denied My name.

1. Thank You, Lord, for something new You are set to do this year.

2. This year, I declare unlimited open doors to endless opportunities. In Jesus' Name, Amen.

3. Father, give me access to great places this year. In Jesus' Name, Amen.

4. Lord, all good and perfect doors You have opened for me shall not be shut. In Jesus' Name, Amen.

5. Father, whatever door the enemies shut against me that are supposed to be open, I command that they be opened now. In Jesus' Name, Amen.

6. Lord, all doors leading to my breakthrough shall be opened for me this year. In Jesus' Name, Amen.

19

It's My Season of Elevation and Promotion

Psalm 75:6 (KJV)

For promotion cometh neither from the east, nor from the west, nor from the south.

1. Thank You, Lord, for answering my prayer and petitions.

2. Father Lord, this year, I am stepping into a new level in my life, marriage and career in Jesus' Name.

3. I decree and declare that this year, I shall not be stagnant. In Jesus' Name, Amen.

4. Father, lift me up to the place and position

You have prepared for me. In Jesus' Name, Amen.

5. O God, all promotions come from You; therefore, take me to the higher ground. In Jesus' Name, Amen.

6. This year, I shall be the head only, and never the tail; above and not beneath. In Jesus' Name, Amen.

7. Today, I reject evil manipulation that wants to keep me perpetually small. In Jesus' Name, Amen.

20

Enlarge My Coast

1 Chronicles 4:10

And Jabez called on the God of Israel saying, "Oh, that You would bless me indeed, and enlarge my territory, that Your hand would be with me, and that You would keep me from evil, that I may not cause pain!" So God granted him what he requested.

1. Father, thank You for answering my prayers and putting my adversaries to shame.

2. Lord, bless me indeed and enlarge my coast. In Jesus' Name, Amen.

3. This year, Father, help me to expand to the right, and to the left, and in all directions. In Jesus' Name, Amen.

4. O Lord, expand my business, career, and ministry this year. In Jesus' Name, Amen.

5. Father, let Your mighty hand rest upon me this year. Whatever I do shall experience exponential increase. In Jesus' Name, Amen.

6. Lord, for Your sake, this year, increase my influence and impact. In Jesus' Name, Amen.

7. I receive grace to conquer more lands and territories for You. In Jesus' Name, Amen.

21

Victory over Spirit of Error

Isaiah 45:2

I will go before thee, and make the crooked places straight: I will break in pieces the gates of brass, and cut in sunder the bars of iron

1. Father, thank You for always answering my prayers.

2. Lord, today, I condemn and remove from my life every spirit that causes me to do wrong and walk in error. In Jesus' Name, Amen.

3. O God of Glory, I block all negative, evil, and demonic voices that want to derail and distract me this year. In Jesus' Name, Amen.

4. Father, I destroy by fire the spirit of confusion in my life and career. It shall not succeed this year. In Jesus' Name, Amen.

5. Lord, I receive a sharp, intelligent and focused mind to achieve all that You have for me this year. In Jesus' Name, Amen.

22

Divine Guidance

Proverbs 19:21

There are many plans in a man's heart,

Nevertheless the Lord's counsel—that will stand.

1. Father, thank You for all that You have done, all that You are doing, and all that You are yet to do.

2. Father, release into my life extraordinary wisdom that will bring forth and show Your glory in my life.

3. Lord, give me the sensitivity of Spirit to do the right thing at the right time.

4. Father, let my word not fall to the ground. Let

everything I do and say have divine support. In Jesus' Name, Amen.

5. Father, may I never be a spectator of Your power, but evidence of Your power with great testimonies in my life. In Jesus' Name, Amen.

6. Holy Spirit, the Spirit of wisdom and knowledge, guide me into greatness, victory and breakthrough this year. In Jesus' Name, Amen.

7. Father, let me not gain speed in the wrong direction this year. In Jesus' Name, Amen.

23

Divine Connections

Isaiah 60:1-3, 16

Arise, shine;
For your light has come!
And the glory of the Lord is risen upon you.
2 For behold, the darkness shall cover the earth,
And deep darkness the people;
But the Lord will arise over you,
And His glory will be seen upon you.
3 The Gentiles shall come to your light,
And kings to the brightness of your rising.
You shall drink the milk of the Gentiles,
16 And milk the breast of kings;
You shall know that I, the Lord, am your Savior
And your Redeemer, the Mighty One of Jacob.

1. You are Lord over the universe. Lord, I declare Your praise and glory.

2. Father, this year, connect me to the promoter and the elevator of my destiny. In Jesus' Name, Amen.

3. Omnipresent God, let me not walk through this year alone; stand with me, Lord; let Your rod and Your staff comfort me on every side. In Jesus' Name, Amen.

4. Father, this year, let me not be in the wrong place at the wrong time; let me not be in the right place at the wrong time. Lord, guide all my steps and lead me. In Jesus' Name, Amen.

5. Father, this year, connect me to those who will enhance my life and make my way easy and fulfilling. In Jesus' Name, Amen.

6. This year, Lord, break down all evil networks and connections positioned to bring me down. In Jesus' Name, Amen.

7. Father Lord, let me dine and drink with kings this year. In Jesus' Name, Amen.

24

No More Profitless Labor

Isaiah 48:17

Thus says the Lord, your Redeemer, The Holy One of Israel: "I am the Lord your God, Who teaches you to profit, Who leads you by the way you should go.

1. Thank You, Lord, for Your kindness and mercy over my life and loved ones.

2. Father, this year, teach me to profit maximally in all my endeavors. In Jesus' Name, Amen.

3. Father, I declare that there will be no more profitless labor in my life. In Jesus' Name, Amen.

4. Lord, I command every spirit of slavery and profitless-ness to bow and move out of my life in Jesus' Name.

5. This year, I rebuke and condemn every spirit that makes me work like an elephant but eat like an ant. In Jesus' Name, Amen.

6. By the power of the Holy Spirit, I shall reap plentifully from all my labors this year. In Jesus' Name, Amen.

7. Father, by grace, I shall not struggle to make it in my business, career and ministry. In Jesus' Name, Amen.

8. Father, let everything about me flourish this year in Jesus' Name.

25

Give Me the Nations

Psalm 2:8

Ask of Me, and I will give You The nations for Your inheritance, And the ends of the earth for Your possession.

1. Father, thank You for all Your blessings that we enjoy.

2. Today, Lord, expand my reach to nations. I refuse to be only a local champion; I am a global entity. In Jesus' Name, Amen.

3. Lord, I take possession of wherever the sole of my foot shall tread upon - Lord, I shall not be limited or restrained to my city of dwelling. In Jesus' Name, Amen.

4. Father, every force in operation to strangle my greatness in this land must be condemned now in Jesus' Name.

5. This year, we declare the opening of nations of the earth for the penetration of the Gospel of our Lord Jesus Christ. In Jesus' Name, Amen.

6. In the name of Jesus, we pray that the kings of various nations of the earth will submit to the Lordship of Jesus and reign. Amen.

7. Lord, this year, let the treasure of the earth open up to me and my family. In Jesus' Name, Amen.

26

Financial Breakthrough

3 John 1:2

Beloved, I pray that you may prosper in all things and be in health, just as your soul prospers.

1. Lord, thank You for giving me the ability and grace to continue to be alive to witness Your goodness.

2. Father, this year, I refuse to be broke financially. In Jesus' Name, Amen.

3. Father, let all financial hardship I experience last year never resurface again. In Jesus' Name, Amen.

4. Father, by the authority of the mighty name of Jesus, I break and destroy all powers limiting

my financial success. Amen.

5. Father, let the floodgates of heaven open up for me this year; let me prosper financially for Your glory. In Jesus' Name, Amen.

6. Lord, endow me with the power to acquire wealth; give me grace to sponsor the gospel. In Jesus' Name, Amen.

7. Father, I pull down strongholds of poverty that want to keep me perpetually poor. In Jesus' Name, Amen.

8. Father, I shall not borrow this year; I receive favor to pay off my debt, then lend to nations. In Jesus' Name, Amen.

27

The Spirit of Excellence

Daniel 6:3

Then this Daniel distinguished himself above the governors and satraps, because an excellent spirit was in him; and the king gave thought to setting him over the whole realm.

1. Father, thank You for Your Holy Spirit that resides in me.

2. Lord, today, I activate the Spirit of excellence to be at work in my life all through this year. In Jesus' Name, Amen.

3. Father, give me the grace to do everything right in Jesus' Name.

4. Father, I come against the demons and forces of error and wrongdoing in Jesus' Name.

5. Lord, I receive the Spirit of excellence for outstanding performance in assignments and purpose in Jesus' Name. Amen.

6. Lord, help me overcome habits and behaviors that sabotage my success in life. In Jesus' Name, Amen.

7. Today, I step into the journey of becoming only the best, and living above and beyond average in Jesus' Name. Amen.

28

Spiritual Discernment

1 Corinthian 12:4-7

There are diversities of gifts, but the same Spirit. There are differences of ministries, but the same Lord. And there are diversities of activities, but it is the same God who works all in all. But the manifestation of the Spirit is given to each one for the profit of all:

1. Thank You, Jesus, for always guiding me with Your word and voice.

2. Father, this year, teach me to know You and hear You more. In Jesus' Name, Amen.

3. Lord, instruct me; let me discern Your direction for my life, family and career. In Jesus' Name, Amen.

4. Father Lord, by Your spirit of knowledge and wisdom, help me to discern right from wrong; let me not fall into error this year. In Jesus' Name, Amen.

5. Holy Spirit, this year, speak to me, reveal Yourself to me, and open my eyes to see the possibilities in what natural man calls impossible. In Jesus' Name, Amen.

6. Spirit of the living God, help me to be sensitive to Your movements and waves this year. In Jesus' Name, Amen.

7. Help me, Lord, to understand time and season this year.

8. Lord, help me to only be in the right place at the right time, and to say the right thing at the right time. In Jesus' Name, Amen.

29

Harvest

Matthew 9:36-38

But when He saw the multitudes, He was moved with compassion for them, because they were weary and scattered, like sheep having no shepherd. Then He said to His disciples, "The harvest truly is plentiful, but the laborers are few. Therefore pray the Lord of the harvest to send out laborers into His harvest."

1. Father, thank You for my life, family and network. Thank You for breathing life into all things that concern me.

2. Lord, this year, I shall harvest all my labor from previous years - now. In Jesus' Name, Amen.

3. Lord, every seed that I have sown or will sow this year will bring forth bounty harvest in Jesus' Name. Amen.

4. Father, You are the rewarder of everyone who diligently seeks You; O Lord, let the rewards of my good deeds come quickly this year. In Jesus' Name, Amen.

5. Father, remove and destroy demonic activities that want to truncate harvest season. In Jesus' Name, Amen.

6. Father, though my beginning is small by your grace and favor, I shall greatly increase this year. In Jesus' Name, Amen.

7. Father, let the earth yield her increase for me and my family this year. In Jesus' Name, Amen.

30

Divine Speed and Acceleration

Isaiah 40:29-31

He gives power to the weak,
And to those who have no might He increases strength.
Even the youths shall faint and be weary,
And the young men shall utterly fall;
But those who wait on the Lord
Shall renew their strength;
They shall mount up with wings like eagles,
They shall run and not be weary,
They shall walk and not faint.

1. Thank You, Lord; You have been so faithful and just. I am grateful that I am a child of God.

2. This year, by the power of the Holy Spirit at work in my life, I declare speed and acceleration. In Jesus' Name, Amen.

3. Father Lord, let my loved ones and I ride on Your wings this year. No limits, no restrictions, and no stagnations. In Jesus' Name, Amen.

4. Father, give me fresh anointing to achieve great things above my expectations. In Jesus' Name, Amen.

5. Father, give me massive success in the areas where I failed last year. In Jesus' Name, Amen.

6. This year, I receive networks of help that will take me places that I have never dreamed. In Jesus' Name, Amen.

7. Father, this year, what will take others ten years to achieve, by Your hands at work in my life, I shall achieve in one year. In Jesus' Name, Amen.

31

My Star Must Shine

Isaiah 60:19-20

"The sun shall no longer be your light by day,

Nor for brightness shall the moon give light to you;

But the Lord will be to you an everlasting light,

And your God your glory.

Your sun shall no longer go down,

Nor shall your moon withdraw itself;

For the Lord will be your everlasting light,

And the days of your mourning shall be ended.

1. Thanks and praises to You, Lord. Your love is like a river, ever-flowing toward me.

2. I have a destiny. I am a born star. My star must shine forth in Jesus' Name. Amen.

3. Father, every evil demonic blanket covering the star of my destiny must catch fire now. In Jesus' Name, Amen.

4. Father, every effort to frustrate my destiny star and that of my children shall not succeed. In Jesus' Name, Amen.

5. Lord, we render null and void all networks of enemies who try to bastardize my glory and greatness this year. In Jesus' Name, Amen.

6. Lord, we arrest by the Holy Ghost all destiny, stars and glory manipulators. In Jesus' Name, Amen.

7. Father, this year, let my light shine brighter and greater than last year. In Jesus' Name, Amen.

8. Father, let me be an outstanding example that would showcase Your glory everywhere I go. In Jesus' Name, Amen.

32

Showers of Blessings

Ezekiel 34:25-27

"I will make a covenant of peace with them, and cause wild beasts to cease from the land; and they will dwell safely in the wilderness and sleep in the woods. I will make them and the places all around my hill a blessing; and I will cause showers to come down in their season; there shall be showers of blessing. Then the trees of the field shall yield their fruit, and the earth shall yield her increase. They shall be safe in their land; and they shall know that I am the Lord, when I have broken the bands of their yoke and delivered them from the hand of those who enslaved them."

1. O Lord, I praise You for all Your innumerable blessings in my life.

2. Today, I declare the blessing of God over this year. This year is blessed in Jesus' Name. Amen.

3. Lord, bless me indeed this year; remove pain, sadness, and frustration from my life. In Jesus' Name, Amen.

4. Father, by the blood of Jesus, let Your blessing override all the curses of the enemies in my life. Amen.

5. I declare, Lord, this is my season for showers of blessing. I shall not be cursed. The powers of the enemies over my life are paralyzed in Jesus' Name. Amen.

6. I declare that my family and the dynasty is blessed. This year, we shall emerge as forces to be reckoned with in Jesus' mighty Name.

7. Father, this year, let the trees of the field yield their fruit, and the earth yield her increase in our lives. In Jesus' Name, Amen.

33

Crushing Barriers and Strongholds

2 Corinthians 10:4-5

For the weapons of our warfare are not carnal but mighty in God for pulling down strongholds, casting down arguments and every high thing that exalts itself against the knowledge of God, bringing every thought into captivity to the obedience of Christ,

1. Father, thank You for helping me to always win in all the battles of life.

2. This year, all barriers and blockages to my success must be crushed in Jesus' Name.

3. Oh Lord, make all crooked paths straight this year in Jesus' Name.

4. Lord of Hosts, every stronghold and all strong enemies against me must fall this year. In Jesus' Name, Amen.

5. This year, I pull down all spiritual and mental strongholds stopping me from fulfilling my destiny. In Jesus' Name, Amen.

6. Father, challenge all challengers of my future glory. In Jesus' Name, Amen.

7. Father, all prolonged, mountainous problems in my life must be leveled this year. In Jesus' Name, Amen.

34

Deliverance from Fear

Psalm 34:4

I sought the LORD, and He heard me,
And delivered me from all my fears.

1. Thank You, Lord, for the trust that I Have in You and Your power to save me.

2. Father, You have not given me the spirit of fear, but of boldness. Therefore, this year, I shall not walk in fear. In Jesus' Name, Amen.

3. Lord, Jesus, I rebuke and cast out every spirit of timidity and fear in my life.

4. This year, I declare I can do all things through Christ who strengthens me. In Jesus' Name, Amen.

5. Father, this year, I refuse to bow or compromise my faith and my unwavering trust in Your power. In Jesus' Name, Amen.

6. This year, I shall fear no evil. No power will be able to overcome me. I am confident in God in my life. In Jesus' Name, Amen.

7. The Lord is my light and my salvation. Whom shall I fear? Therefore, all my enemies who come against me this year will perish completely. In Jesus' Name, Amen.

35

Evil Attacks

Psalm 91:9-11

Because you have made the LORD, who is my refuge,
Even the Most High, your dwelling place,
No evil shall befall you,
Nor shall any plague come near your dwelling;
For He shall give His angels charge over you,
To keep you in all your ways.

1. Thank You, Lord, for Your protection that's always with me.

2. Father, I declare no weapon fashioned against my loved one and I shall prosper. In Jesus' mighty Name, Amen.

3. Father, all arrows of attack against my life and family shall be intercepted by the Holy Ghost. In Jesus' Name, Amen.

4. I declare, no evil shall befall me; no calamity shall come to my dwelling. In Jesus' Name, Amen.

5. Lord, this year, I shall not be a victim of satanic, evil plots. In Jesus' Name, Amen.

6. Father, let all arrows of destruction against me and my family backfire. In Jesus' Name, Amen.

7. This year, my household is shielded by the fire of the Holy Ghost and the Blood of Jesus. Amen.

36

Healing in my Body

Exodus 15:26

and said, "If you diligently heed the voice of the LORD your God and do what is right in His sight, give ear to His commandments and keep all His statutes, I will put none of the diseases on you which I have brought on the Egyptians. For I am the LORD who heals you."

1. Father, save me and I will be saved; heal me and I will be healed.

2. I command every sickness and disease in my body to bow and go, by the power of the Holy Spirit. In Jesus' Name, Amen.

3. Lord, I declare that any infirmity or infection in my body will be rooted out. In Jesus' Name, Amen.

4. Father, release Your miraculous power for healing and freedom from the captivity of sickness. In Jesus' Name, Amen.

5. Father, turn my sorrow to joy, and my mourning into dancing this year. In Jesus' Name, Amen.

6. By the anointing, let every yoke and curse of terminal sickness be destroyed in the name of Jesus. Amen.

7. This year, I shall live my life in divine health, peace and strength. In Jesus' Name, Amen.

37

Intimacy with God

Psalm 63:1

O God, You are my God;
Early will I seek You;
My soul thirsts for You;
My flesh longs for You
In a dry and thirsty land
Where there is no water.

1. Thank You, Jesus, for Your power and glory revealed in my life.

2. Lord, I receive grace to tarry in Your presence - fellowshipping with You in prayer and supplication. In Jesus' Name, Amen.

3. Father, forgive all my sins, disobedience and rebellion toward Your will. In Jesus' Name, Amen.

4. Lord, I surrender to You and Your will; help me to grow in grace and in faith. In Jesus' Name, Amen.

5. Lord, I want to know You more, and the power of Your resurrection, and the fellowship of Your suffering. In Jesus' Name, Amen.

6. Father, give me the grace to dwell in Your word - to study, meditate and apply Your word to my life. In Jesus' Name, Amen.

7. I adore You, Lord; I worship Your majesty. You are the Pillar that holds my life together.

38

Victory for my Head

Psalm 3:3

But You, O LORD, are a shield for me,
My glory and the One who lifts up my head.

1. Thank You, Lord, for Your tremendous blessings in my life.

2. Lord, You are the glory and the lifter of my head. Let my head showcase Your glory. In Jesus' Name, Amen.

3. This year, I declare that my head shall not reject blessings and favor. In Jesus' Name, Amen.

4. Father, deliver my head and mind from evil attacks, mental digression, and loss of memory in Jesus' Name. Amen.

5. I declare that my head shall not be buried or vandalized. In Jesus' Name, Amen.

6. O Lord, this year, my head will be more powerful and stronger than my enemies. In Jesus' Name, Amen.

7. I declare, I shall be the head and not the tail; above only, and not beneath. In Jesus' Name, Amen.

39

Prayer for My Children

Isaiah 8:18

Here am I and the children whom the LORD has given me!
We are for signs and wonders in Israel
From the LORD of hosts,
Who dwells in Mount Zion.

1. Lord, thank You for granting me all-around favor and mercies.

2. I and the children the Lord gave me are for signs and wonders. I declare that my children will do amazing things for God's glory in their generation. In Jesus' Name, Amen.

3. This year, the hand of God is upon my children; no evil power will succeed over their lives. In Jesus' Name, Amen.

4. Oh Lord, keep my children in perfect peace in their souls and minds. In Jesus' Name, Amen.

5. Father, this year, let my children succeed in all their academics and studies. In Jesus' Name, Amen.

6. Father, release upon my children the Spirit of excellence; let them stand out among their peers. In Jesus' Name, Amen.

7. Father, my children will fulfill their destiny. They will also serve You all their lives. In Jesus' Name, Amen.

40

Family Issues

Psalm 128:2-4

When you eat the labor of your hands,
You shall be happy, and it shall be well with you.
Your wife shall be like a fruitful vine
In the very heart of your house,
Your children like olive plants
All around your table.
Behold, thus shall the man be blessed
Who fears the LORD.

1. Lord, thank You for my family, and marriage. In Jesus' Name, Amen.

2. Father, I destroy by fire every spirit of

barrenness and miscarriage in my family. I command fruitfulness to reign in my family in Jesus' Name. Amen.

3. Father, You said I will be saved with my household. Please save every unsaved member of my family; let them have a personal relationship with You. In Jesus' Name, Amen.

4. Father, let my family laugh at last; make us a role model of righteousness in this generation. In Jesus' Name, Amen.

5. I renounce and cancel division, divorce, or separation in my family in Jesus' Name. Amen.

6. Father, let peace, love and joy prevail in my marriage. In Jesus' Name, Amen.

7. I come against all anti-marriage spirit operating in this generation. In Jesus' Name, Amen.

41

Marital Issues for Singles

Proverbs 18:22

He who finds a wife finds a good thing,

And obtains favor from the LORD.

1. Father, this year, let there be open doors for me and all the singles that are at the marriageable age in my family, church, and community, in the mighty name of Jesus.

2. Father, wherever my spouse/my life partner may be; let him or her locate me NOW. In Jesus' Name, Amen.

3. Father Lord, I reject disappointment and delay in marriage in the mighty name of Jesus.

4. Father, because two are better than one, I curse all curses of undesired and prolonged single living in my life by the blood of Jesus.

5. Father, paralyze every power that says I will be single throughout my life. In Jesus' Name, Amen.

6. I come against all anti-marriage spirits operating in this generation. In Jesus' Name, Amen.

42

Breaking Curses and Spells

Proverbs 26:2 (NLT)

Like a fluttering sparrow or a darting swallow, an undeserved curse will not land on its intended victim.

1. If God be for me, who can be against me?

2. Lord, by the blood of Jesus, every curse of life operating in my life must be broken and shattered in Jesus' Name. Amen.

3. Every curse, spell, or mark released against me, standing as strongholds in my life, I render them impotent now in Jesus' Name. Amen.

4. Father, this year, I defeat the strongholds of

fear, disappointment, delay, and frustration in my life in Jesus' Name. Amen.

5. Lord, remove and erase whatever represents generational and ancestral curses in my life. In Jesus' Name, Amen.

6. Father, I reverse and renounce all negative and evil pronouncements, incantations, and prophecies concerning me this year in Jesus' Name. Amen.

7. Lord, I destroy the root of any covenants with the devil and his network in Jesus' Name. Amen. (Covenant with premature death, covenant with failure in life, covenant with bad luck and frustration, etc.)

43

Dominion Over Circumstances

Philippians 2:9-11

Therefore God also has highly exalted Him and given Him the name which is above every name, [10] that at the name of Jesus every knee should bow, of those in heaven, and of those on earth, and of those under the earth, [11] and that every tongue should confess that Jesus Christ is Lord, to the glory of God the Father.

1. I thank You, Jesus, for power and authority.

2. I have power and authority over situations and circumstances in Jesus' Name.

3. In the name of Jesus, every knee must bow; therefore, everything troubling me and my

loved ones must bow this year.

4. I declare I have dominion over sickness; I have dominion over poverty; I have dominion over the powers of my enemies. In Jesus' Name, Amen.

5. Lord, I command strangers and foreigners who have come to afflict me to get out of my life now. In Jesus' Name, Amen.

6. Father, let the fire of the Holy Ghost consume all evil and demonic spirits tormenting my family. In Jesus' Name, Amen.

7. This year, satan and his messengers are under my feet. In Jesus' Name, Amen.

44

Divine Protection

Psalm 121:7-8

The LORD shall preserve you from all evil;
He shall preserve your soul.
The LORD shall preserve your going out and your coming in
From this time forth, and even forevermore.

1. Lord, protect my life from the mouth of lions anxious to eat up my flesh this year. In the name of Jesus, Amen.

2. Father, this year, I shall not be a victim of calamity, accidents and devastations. In Jesus' Name, Amen.

3. Lord Jesus, release Your angels to guide me this year and all the days of my life.

4. Father, I rebuke every evil and wickedness released from the satanic kingdom to attack me and my family. In Jesus' Name, Amen.

5. I am covered with the blood of Jesus; I declare that no evil will be mentioned in my dwelling place. In Jesus' Name, Amen.

6. Father, the Bible says, "Touch not my anointed, and do my prophets no harm." Therefore, Lord, make me untouchable to the enemies this year. In Jesus' Name, Amen.

7. Lord, hide me under Your pavilion of heaven where sickness, diseases, and evil cannot reach. In Jesus' Name, Amen.

45

Restorations

Joel 2:25

"So I will restore to you the years that the swarming locust has eaten,

The crawling locust,

The consuming locust,

And the chewing locust,

My great army which I sent among you.

1. Thank You, God of Restoration.
2. Father, let there be divine restoration in my life in Jesus' Name. Amen.
3. Lord, whatever I have lost in previous years, I receive them back in hundred-folds in Jesus' Name. Amen.

4. Oh God of Restoration, I recover all my losses - financial, marital, materials, and others in Jesus' Name. Amen.

5. Father, this year, turn around my captivities above and beyond my expectations in Jesus' Name. Amen.

6. Father, let those who think I am finished or who no longer hope for me come and rejoice with me this year in Jesus' Name. Amen.

7. Father, give me double for all my troubles and setbacks. In Jesus' Name, Amen.

46

Overflow of Provision

Psalm 23:5

*You prepare a feast for me
in the presence of my enemies.
You honor me by anointing my head with oil.
My cup overflows with blessings.*

1. Father, I thank You for providing for all my needs according to Your riches, in glory through Christ Jesus.

2. Father, let my cup overflow; Lord, give me more than enough, and make me a blessing to the nations. In Jesus' Name, Amen.

3. Father, release the abundance of heaven in my direction, and open up the treasures of the earth in my favor this year in Jesus' Name.

4. Father, give me the grace to be obedient to Your word in the area of tithing, giving, and generosity toward Your kingdom, in the Name of Jesus.

5. Father, this is not the end of the road for my life; increase me more and more. In Jesus' Name, Amen.

6. I declare that I shall lend to nations; I shall not borrow; I shall not beg from my enemy. In the name of Jesus, Amen.

7. This year, I shall receive everything I need and more to fulfil God's plans and purposes for my life and family. In Jesus' Name, Amen.

47

Supernatural Manifestations and Results

Ephessians 3:20

Now to Him who is able to do exceedingly abundantly above all that we ask or think, according to the power that works in us,

1. Father, thank You for the supply of Your power and Your Spirit.

2. Lord, this year, let Your supernatural power be visible and tangible in all my endeavors.

3. Father, I bring to subjection my flesh, my wisdom, and ego, so that You can have complete control this year in Jesus' Name. Let me not stand in Your way, oh Lord.

4. God of Wonders, this year, manifest Your wondrous work in my family, ministry and business/career. In Jesus' Name, Amen.

5. Lord, use me to do miracles, to heal the broken-hearted, and to bring supernatural change to the lives of those who come in contact with me this year. In Jesus' Name, Amen.

6. Father, by Your supernatural influence in my life, I shall not be ordinary nor do ordinary things this year. In Jesus' Name, Amen.

7. God of glory, let Your mighty hand rest upon me and be seen in all that represents me this year. In Jesus' Name, Amen.

48

Revival

Habakkuk 3:2

O LORD, I have heard Your speech and was afraid;
O LORD, revive Your work in the midst of the years!
In the midst of the years make it known;
In wrath remember mercy.

1. Thank You, Lord, for Your powerful movement of the Spirit all over the world.

2. Father, revive Your work in the midst of this year. In Jesus' Name, Amen.

3. Father Lord, let there be an outpouring of Your Spirit upon all flesh; let the young ones begin to see visions of heaven, and the old ones dream dreams. In Jesus' Name, Amen.

4. Lord, raise up an army all over the world that will be involved in massive evangelism. Jesus, we pray for massive soul-winning and additions to God's kingdom. In Jesus' Name, Amen.

5. Father, we paralyze all evil powers, anti-Christ activities, and Christian persecution all over the world. In Jesus' Name, Amen.

6. Father, bring an awakening into Your Church. Let the church arise from sleep and slumber into the new movement of Your supernatural flow, and Your agenda.

7. Father Lord, we pray that the governments, authorities, and law-makers of nations will do the will of God in Jesus' Name. Amen.

49

Commanding Greatness

Genesis 12:2-3

"I will make you a great nation;
I will bless you
And make your name great;
And you shall be a blessing.
I will bless those who bless you,
And I will curse him who curses you;
And in you all the families of the earth shall be blessed."

1. Thank You, Lord, for Your plan, which is of good and not of evil, to give me an expected end. Thank You for Your plans and purposes for my life, and for the seed of greatness You planted in me.

2. Father, change my destiny for the better, transform my life, and establish me in Your greatness this year. In Jesus' Name, Amen.

3. Father, by the covenant of Abraham at work in my life, I receive grace to walk in greatness and enter into great places. In Jesus' Name, Amen.

4. Father, make my name great, and make my dynasty as a great nation. In Jesus' Name, Amen.

5. Father, I come against every delay and setback in my destiny this year. In Jesus' Name, Amen.

6. Father, bring to manifestation all prophetic words of blessings spoken about my life, beginning with this year. In Jesus' Name, Amen.

7. Father, I have no power of my own. I can only do all things through You. Therefore, strengthen me with the knowledge, wisdom, and creativity to realize all my dreams this year in Jesus' Name. Amen.

50

Anointing of the Holy Spirit

Micah 3:8

But truly I am full of power by the spirit of the LORD, and of judgment, and of might, to declare unto Jacob his transgression, and to Israel his sin.

1. Holy Spirit of the living God, come upon me afresh. In Jesus' Name, Amen.

2. Father Lord, empower me by Your anointing; move me from ordinary to extraordinary; from natural to supernatural, in Jesus' Name.

3. Lord, let the power of the Almighty come upon me and overshadow me. In Jesus' Name, Amen.

4. Holy Spirit, let Your fire burn in me; let me be of service to You more, with renewed strength and zeal. In Jesus' Name, Amen.

5. When the anointing came upon David, he was transformed to another man. Father, transform my destiny by Your anointing; let my life make an impact in Your Kingdom this year. In Jesus' Name, Amen.

6. I receive the boldness and confidence from the Holy Spirit to preach the gospel and evangelize the world. In Jesus' Name, Amen.

7. By Your Spirit, let everything that comes into contact with me receive life. In Jesus' Name, Amen.

51

No More Shame

Isaiah 61:7

*Instead of your shame you shall have double honor,
And instead of confusion they shall rejoice in their portion.*

*Therefore in their land they shall possess double;
Everlasting joy shall be theirs.*

1. Thank You, Lord, for fighting for me.

2. Lord Jesus, I declare there will be no more shame or reproach in my life this year. In Jesus' Name, Amen.

3. Father, instead of my shame, I shall have double honor, favor and glory. In Jesus' Name, Amen.

4. Every power plotting my failure and every mockery shall be disappointed by the power of God. In Jesus' Name, Amen.

5. According to Psalm 35:4: Let those be put to shame and brought to dishonor who seek after my life; Let those be turned back and brought to confusion who plot my hurt. In Jesus' Name, Amen.

6. Father, I shall end this year with laughter, dancing and celebration, in Jesus' Name.

52

A New Song

Psalm 40:2-3

He also brought me up out of a horrible pit,
Out of the miry clay,
And set my feet upon a rock,
And established my steps.
He has put a new song in my mouth—
Praise to our God;
Many will see it and fear,
And will trust in the Lord.

1. Thank You, Lord, for You are ever with me.

2. Lord, I thank You because I will finish this year better and bigger than I began it. My life shall be full of testimonies and miracles. In Jesus' Name, Amen.

3. Father, this year, put a new song in my life. Turn my life around and let those who see me praise Your Name.

4. Jesus, confirm and establish all that concerns me and my loved ones this year. Let every step I take this year lead to great testimonies that will usher in a new song. In Jesus' Name, Amen.

5. Lord, give me pleasant surprises this year in Jesus' Name. Amen.

6. Father, I will not have a reason to be sad and depressed, or to mourn any members of my family. I declare that there shall be no premature death in our house this year. In Jesus' Name, Amen.

7. We declare a peaceful and joyful year, in the mighty Name of Jesus!

www.ingramcontent.com/pod-product-compliance
Lightning Source LLC
Chambersburg PA
CBHW060333050426
42449CB00011B/2742